Wonderful Singapore
Adult Coloring Book

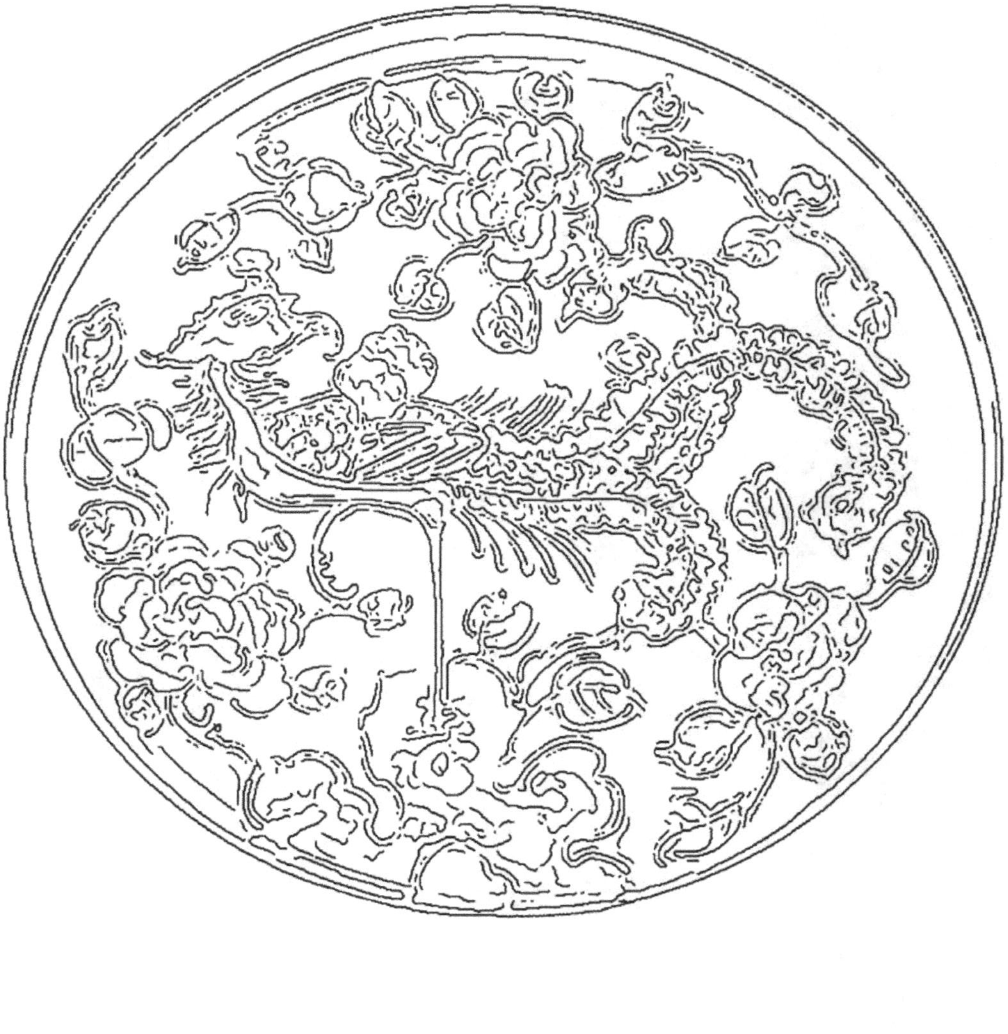

Just Sketch Publishing

Wonderful Singapore
Adult Coloring Book

Copyright: Published in the United States by Just Sketch Publishing
Published January 2017

ISBN-13: 978-1542456913
ISBN-10: 1542456916

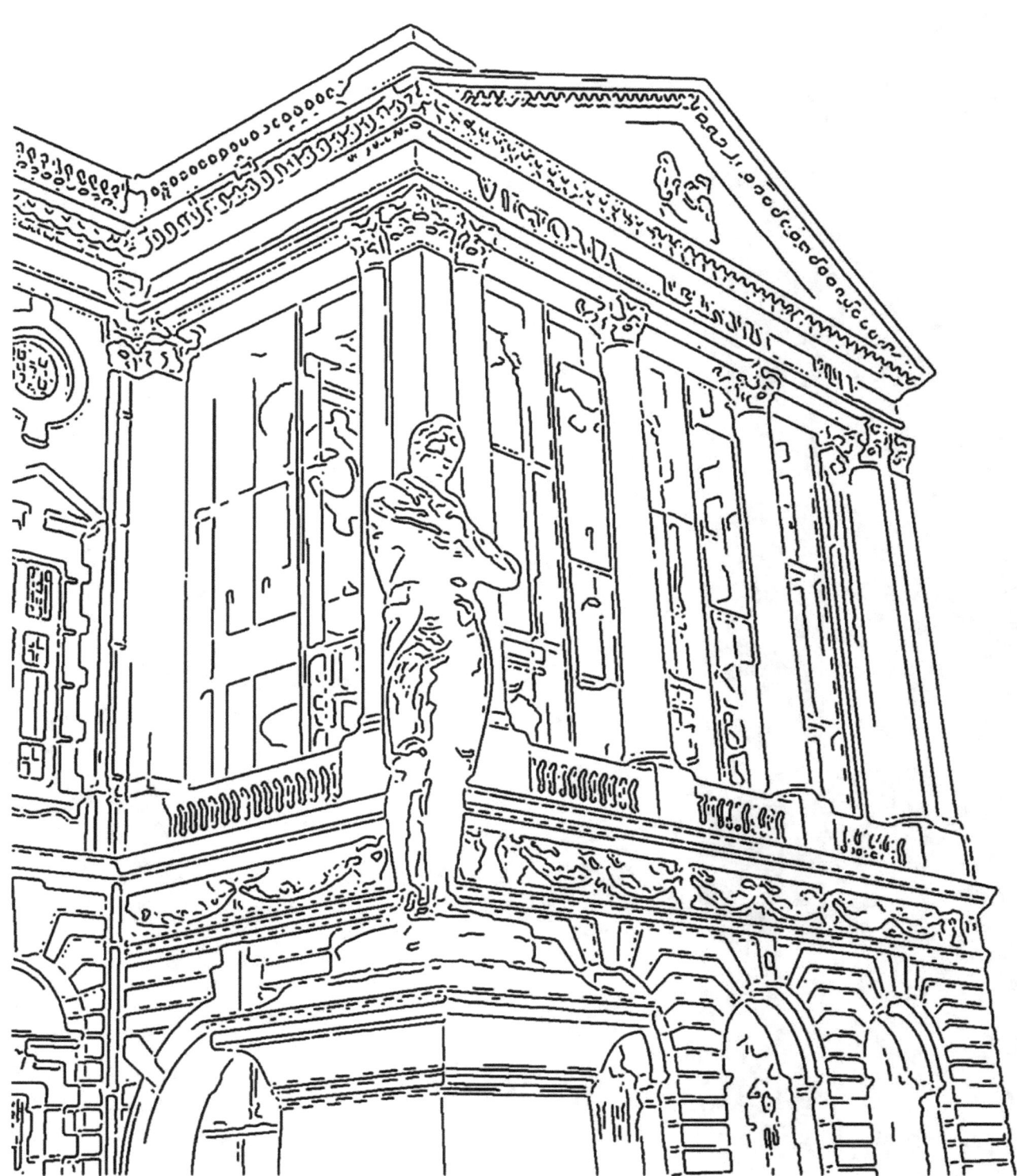

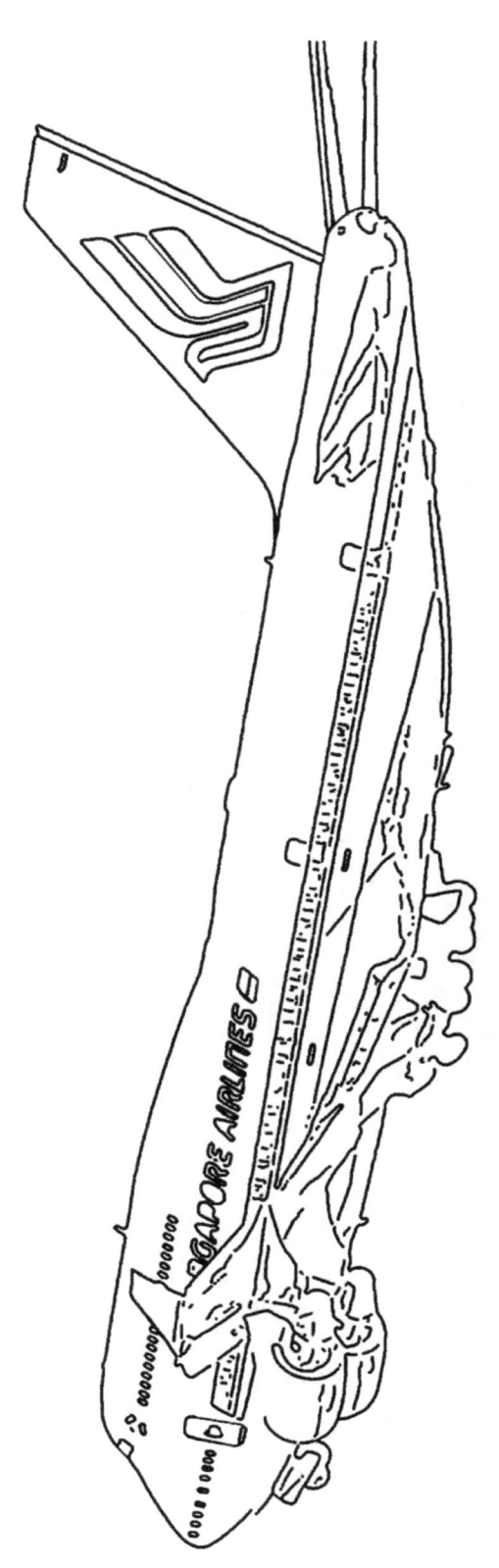

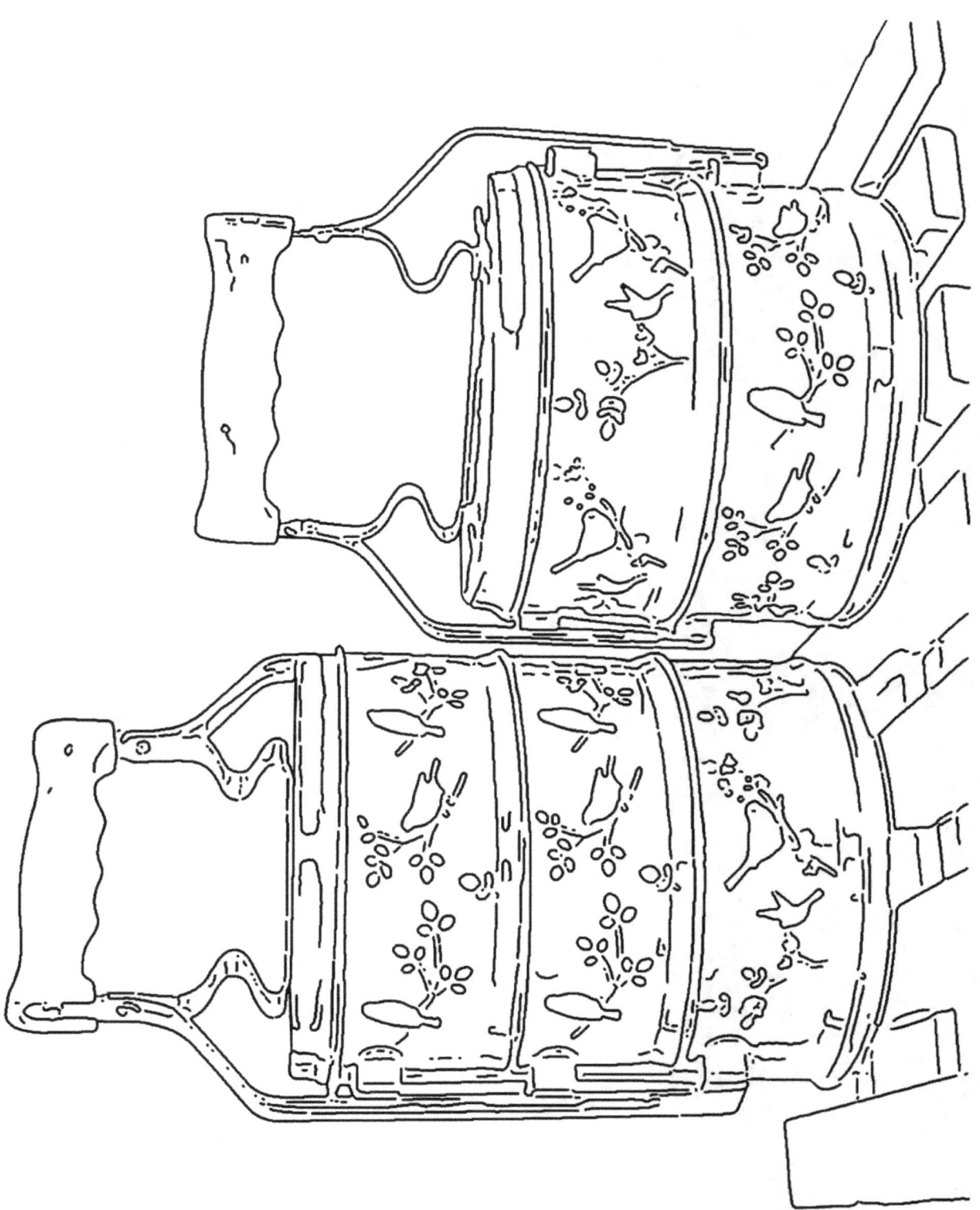

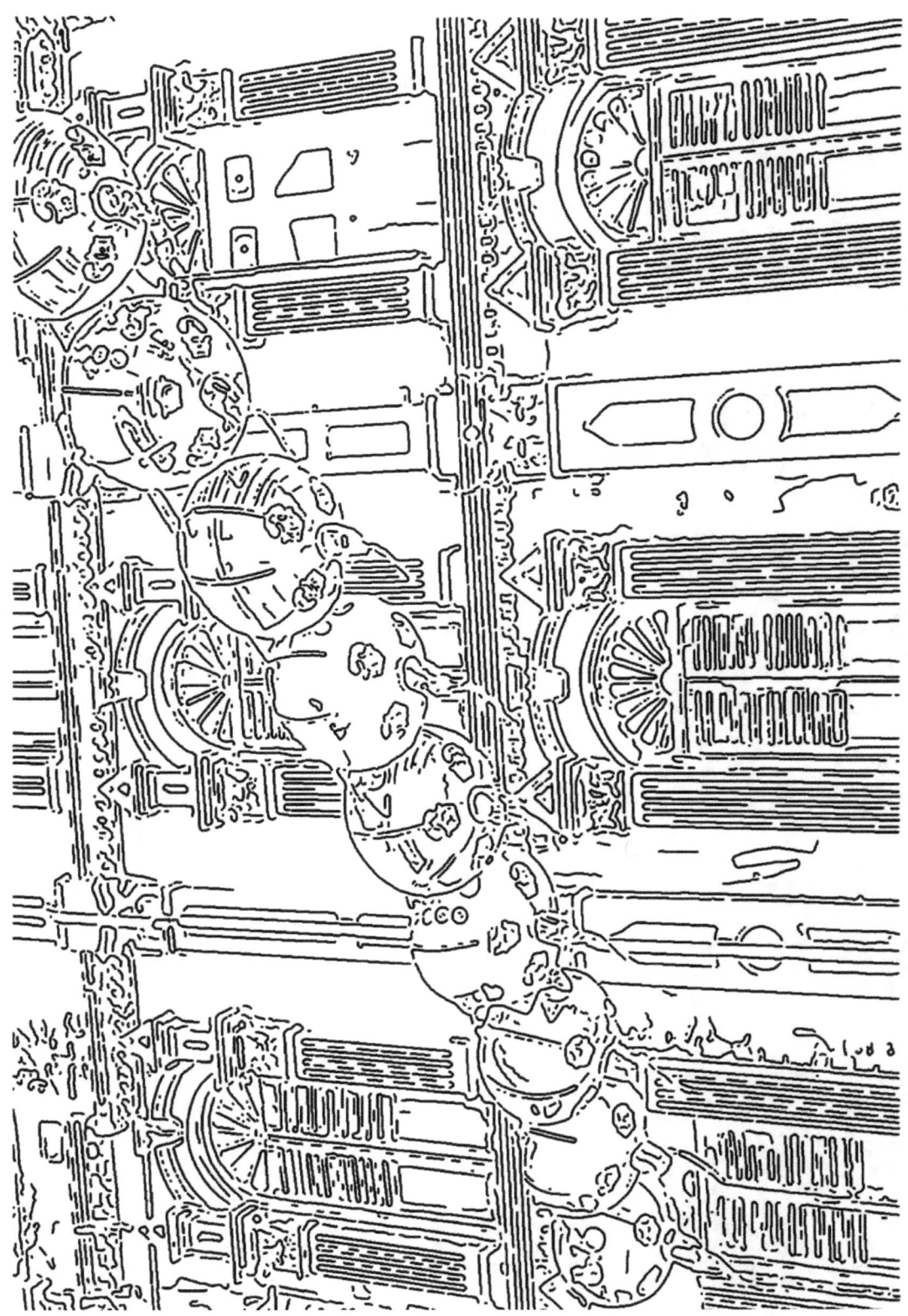

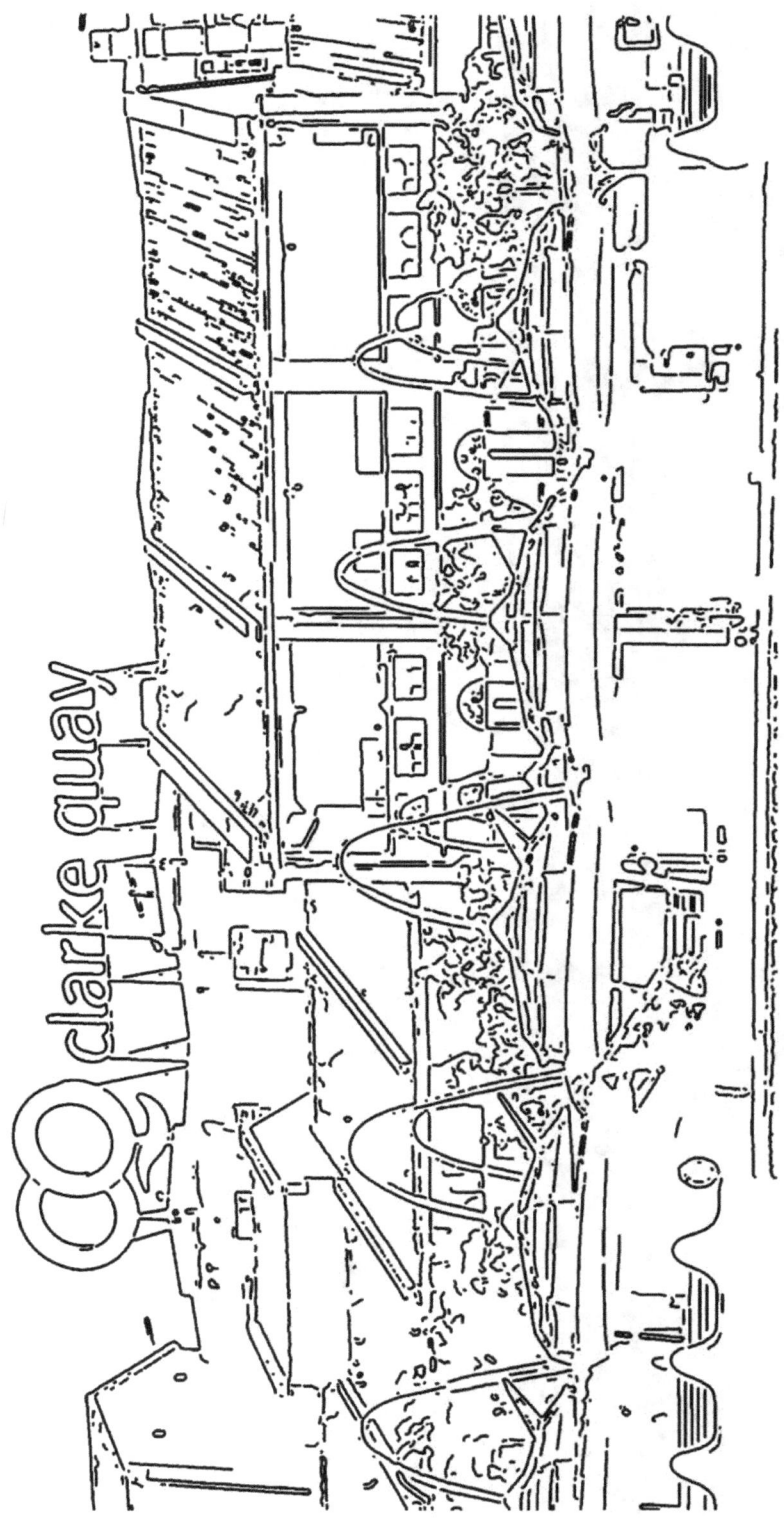

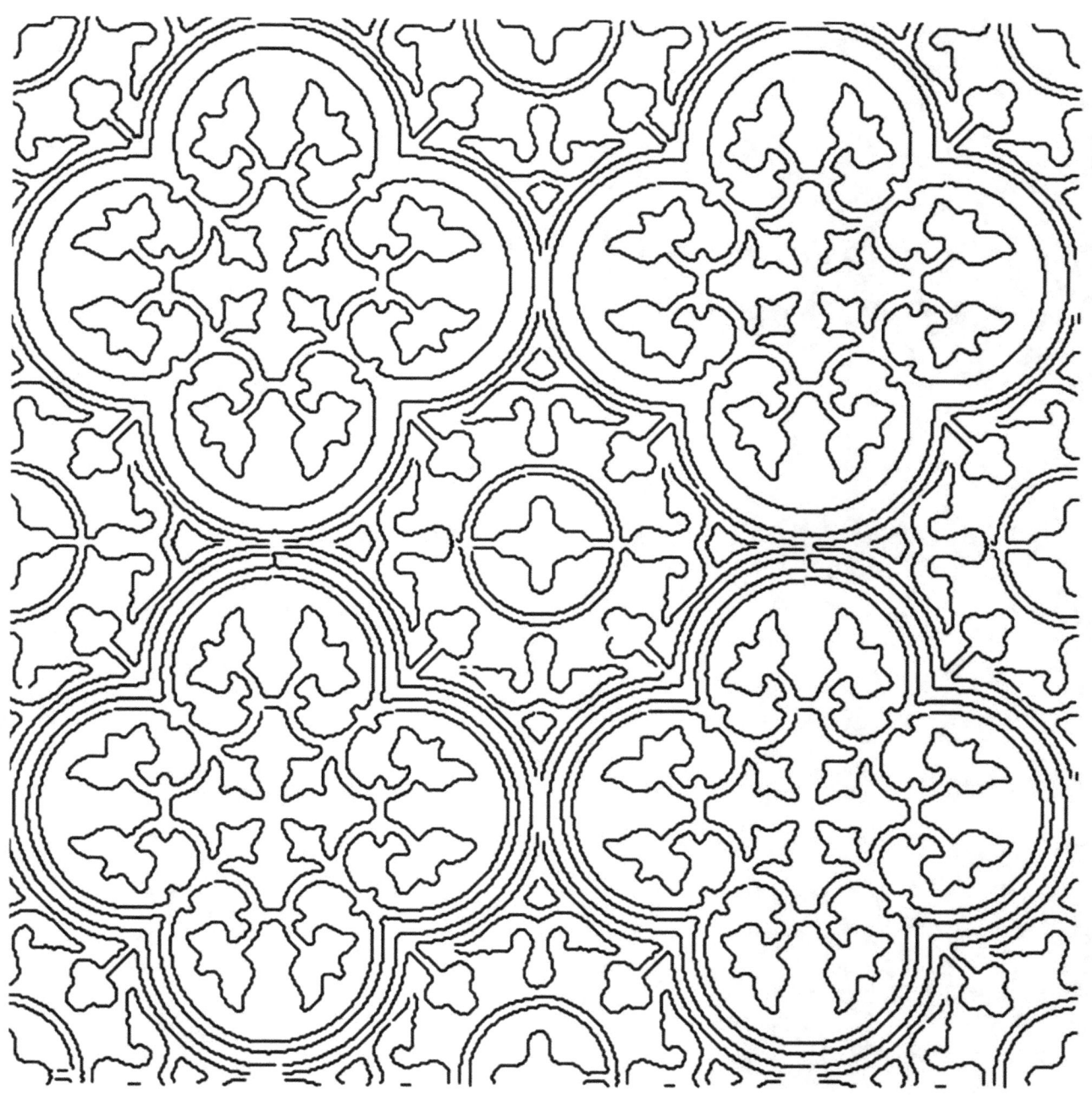

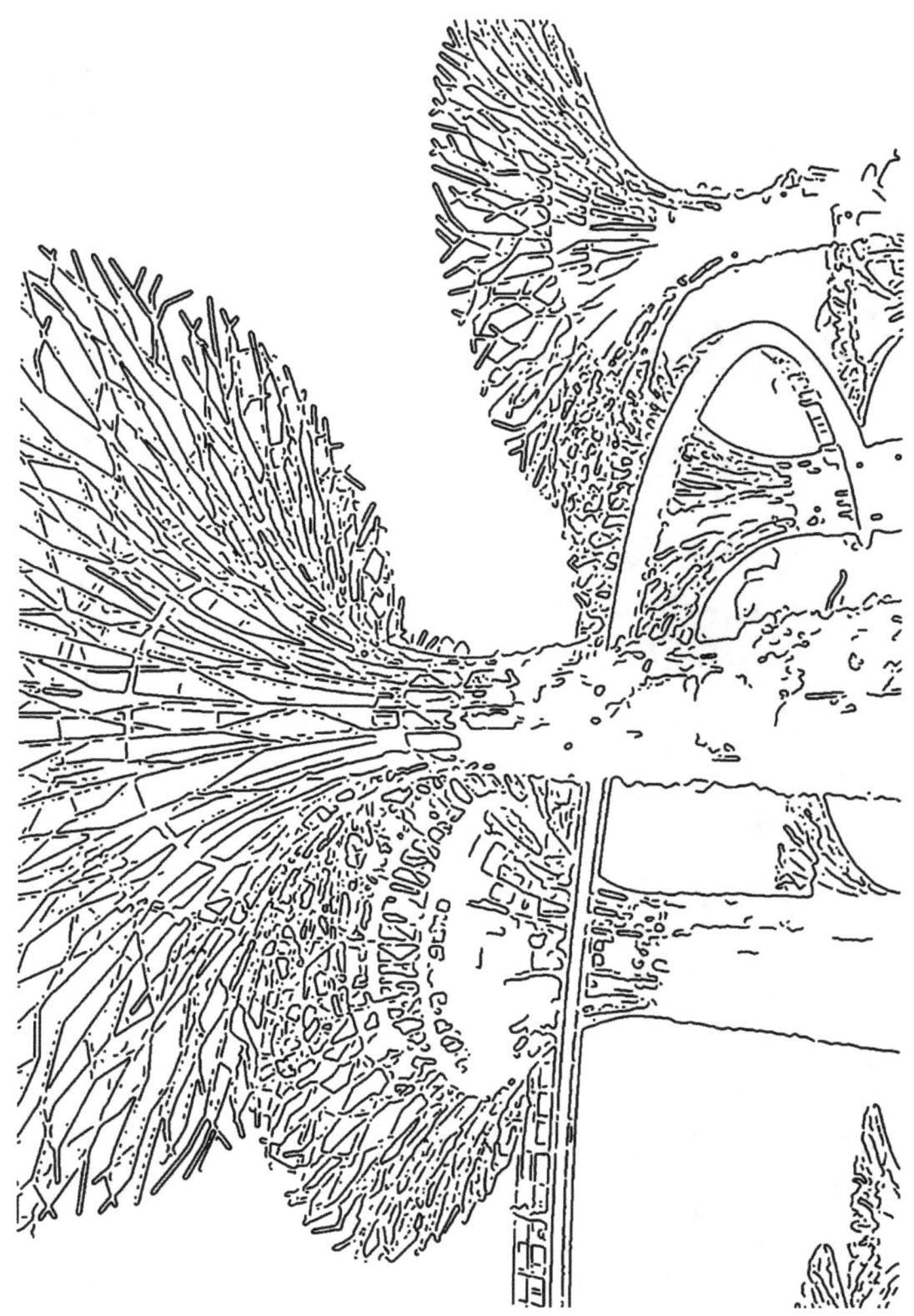

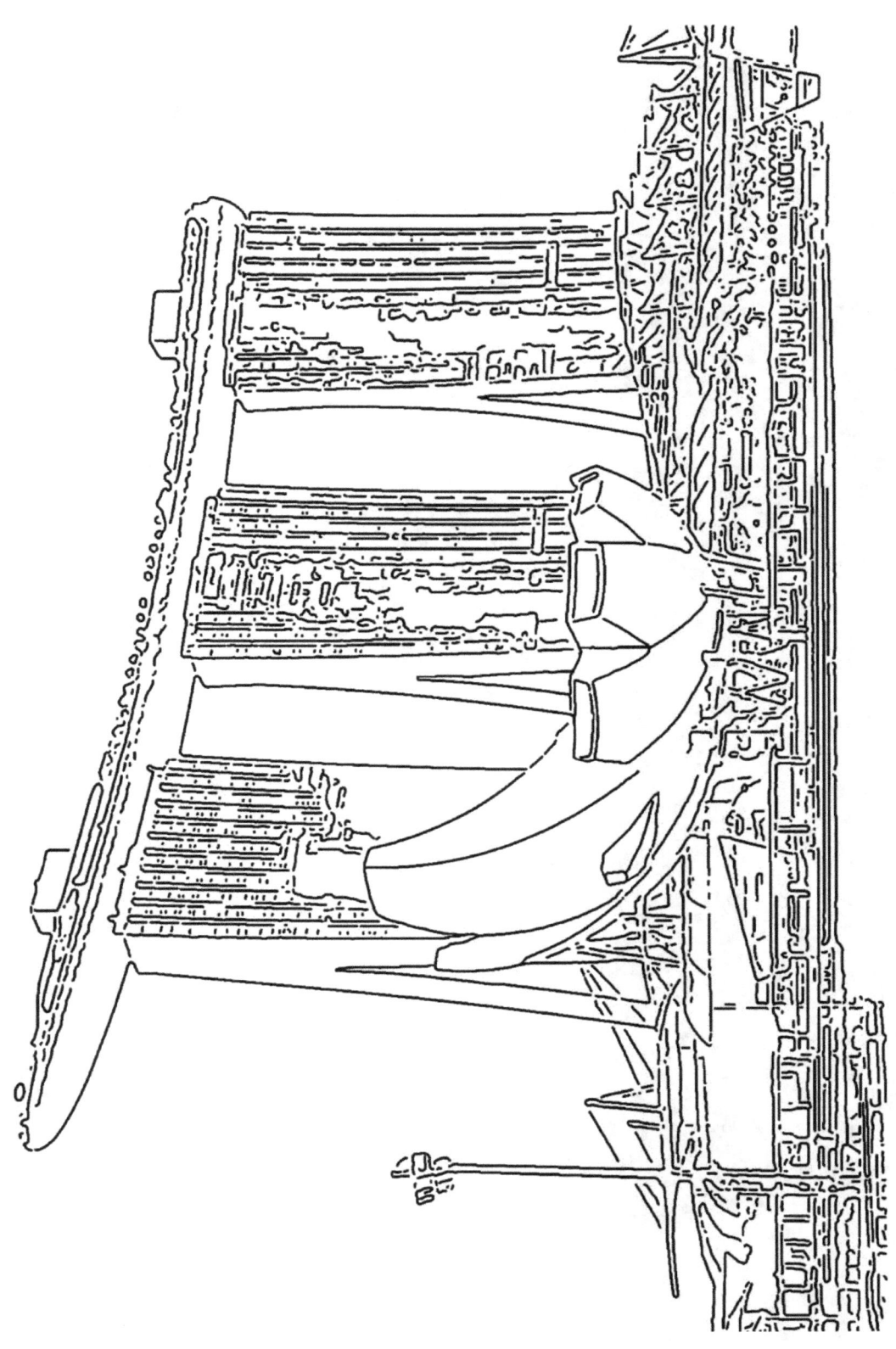

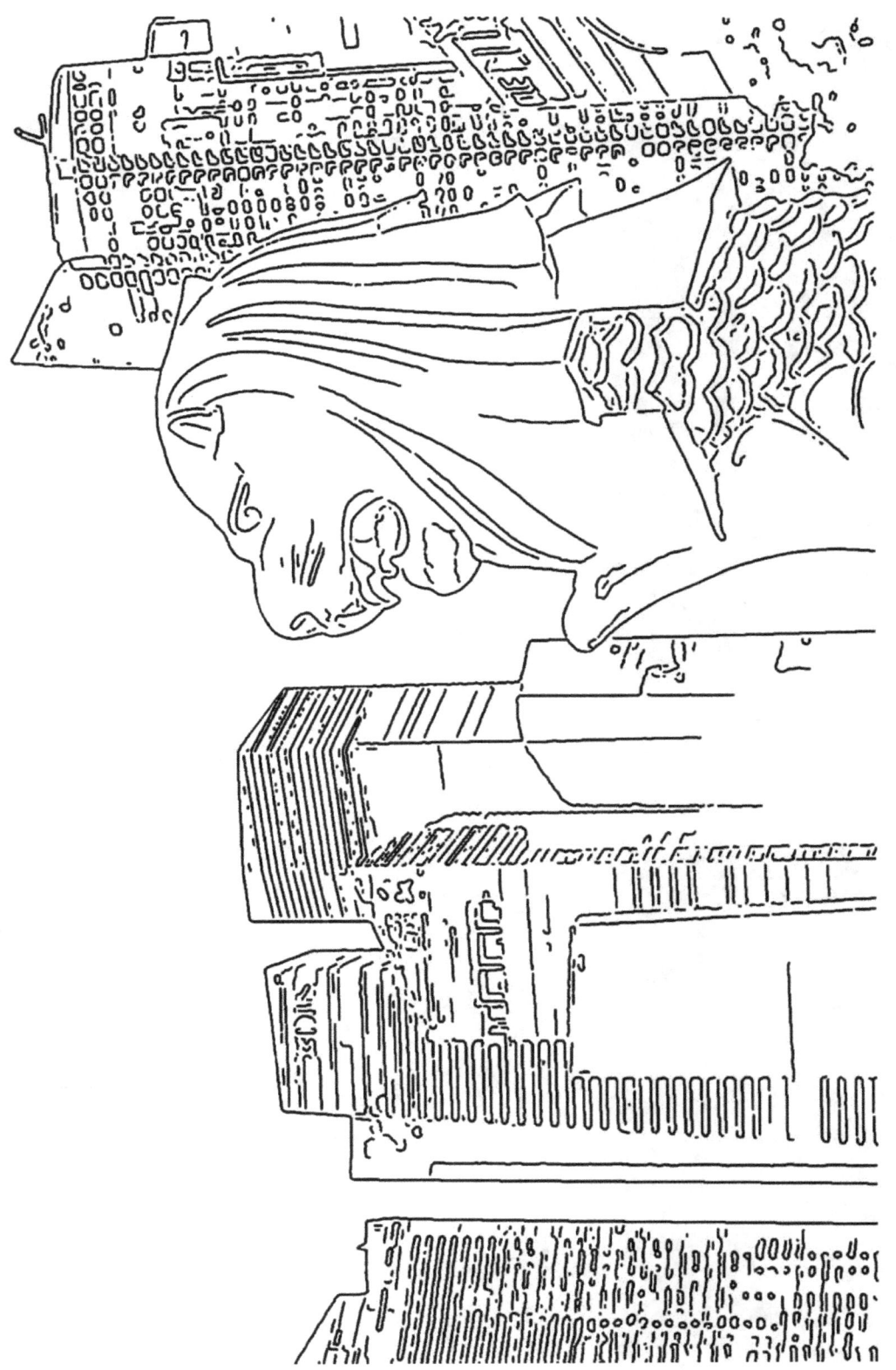

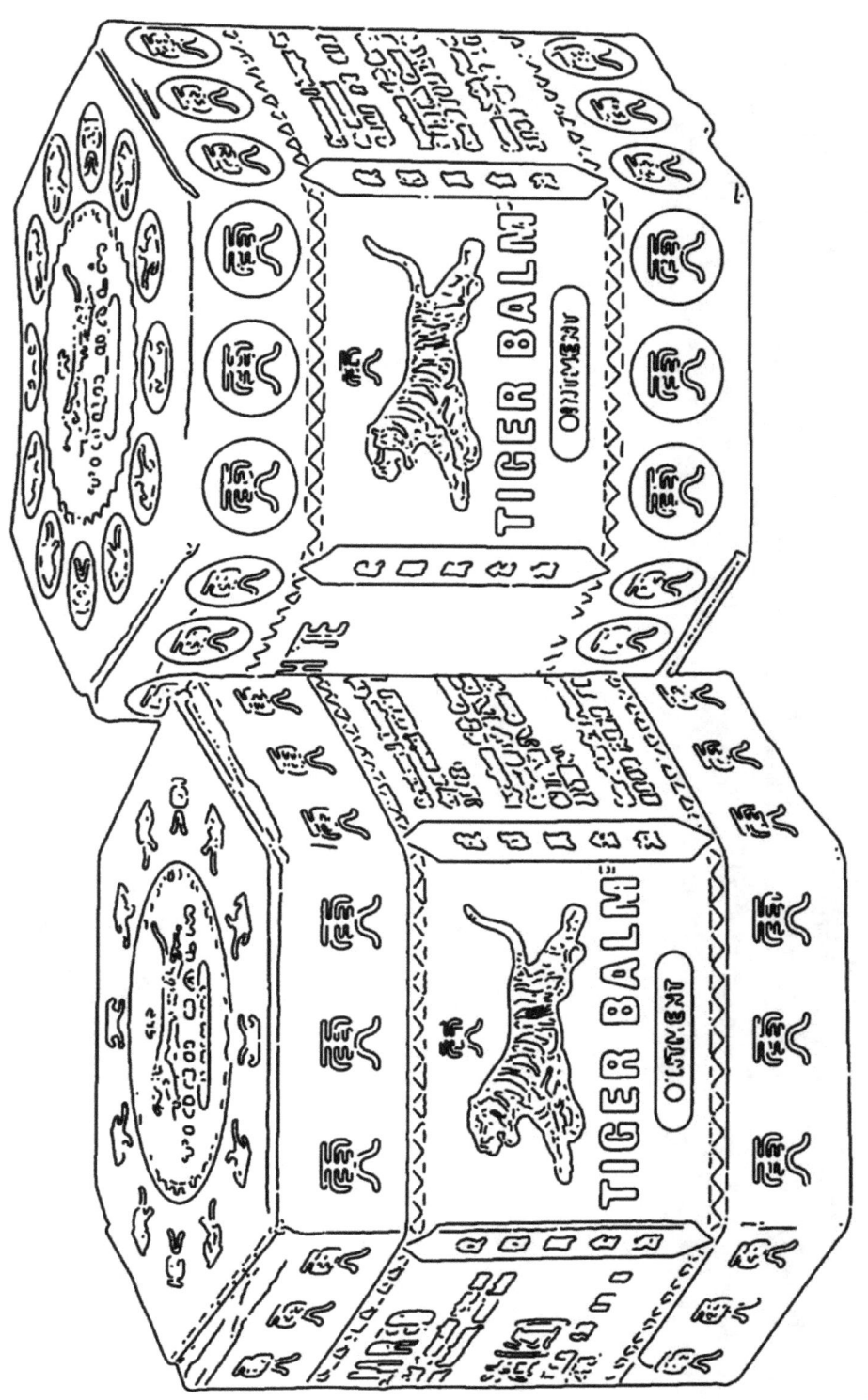

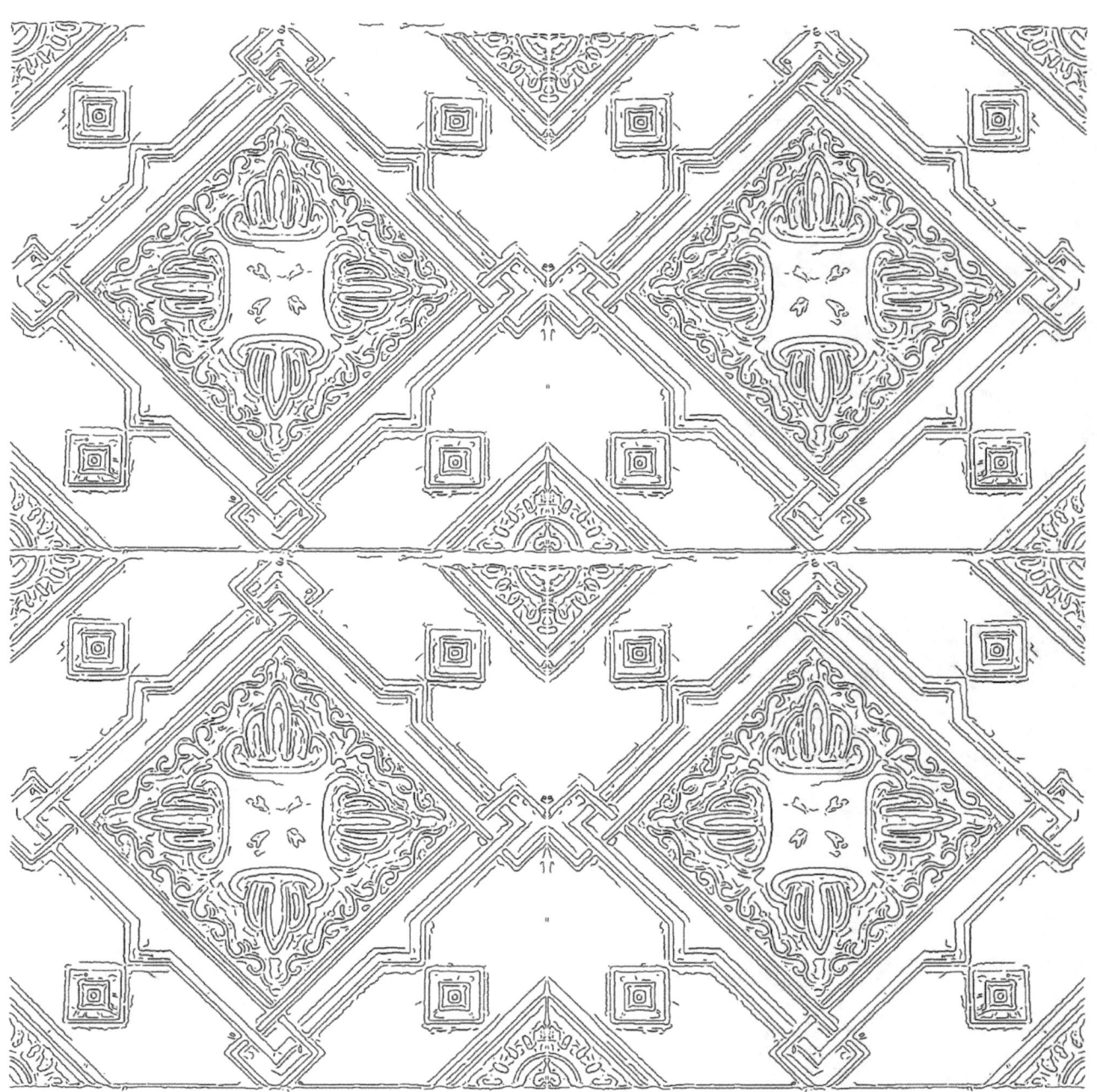

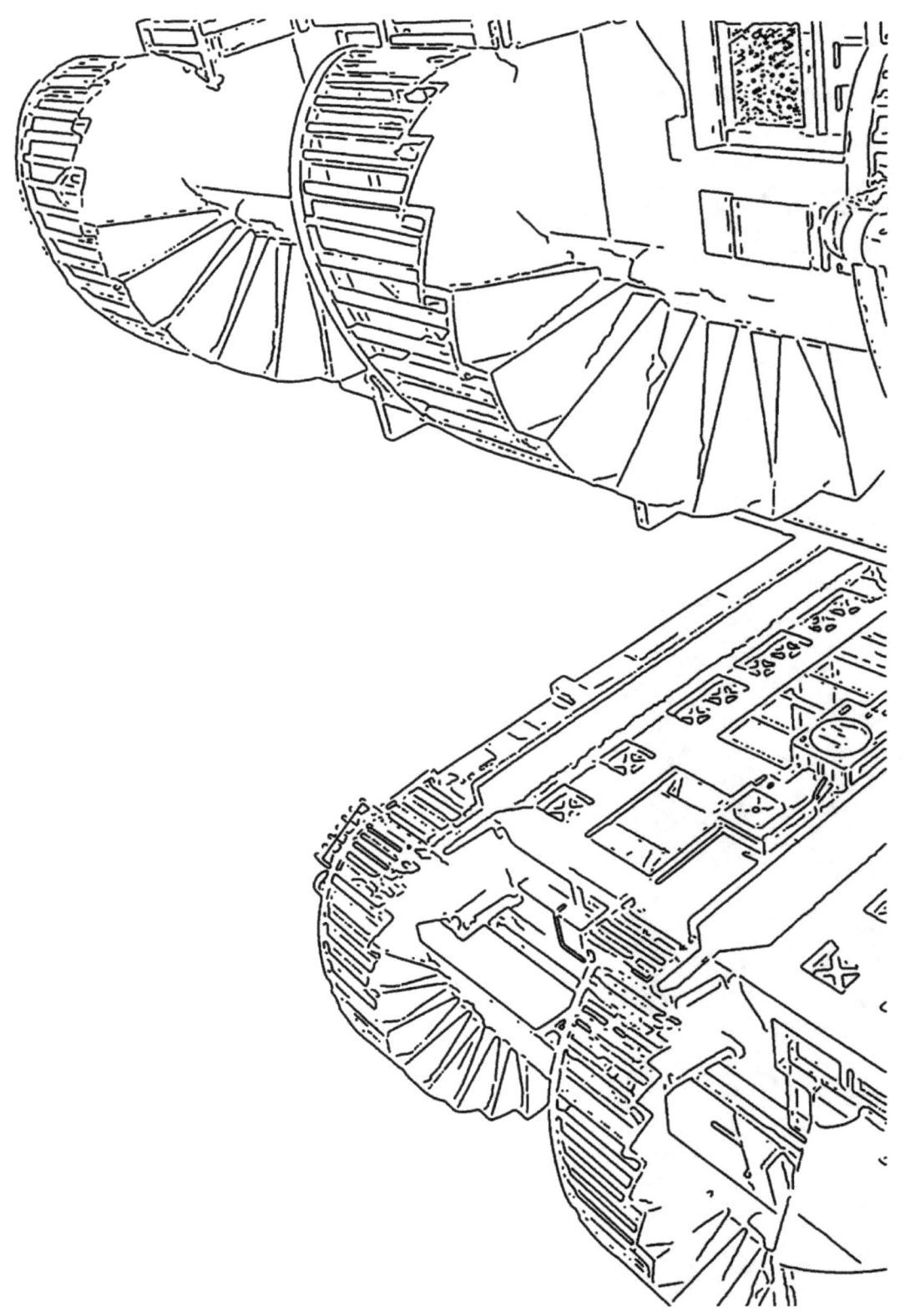

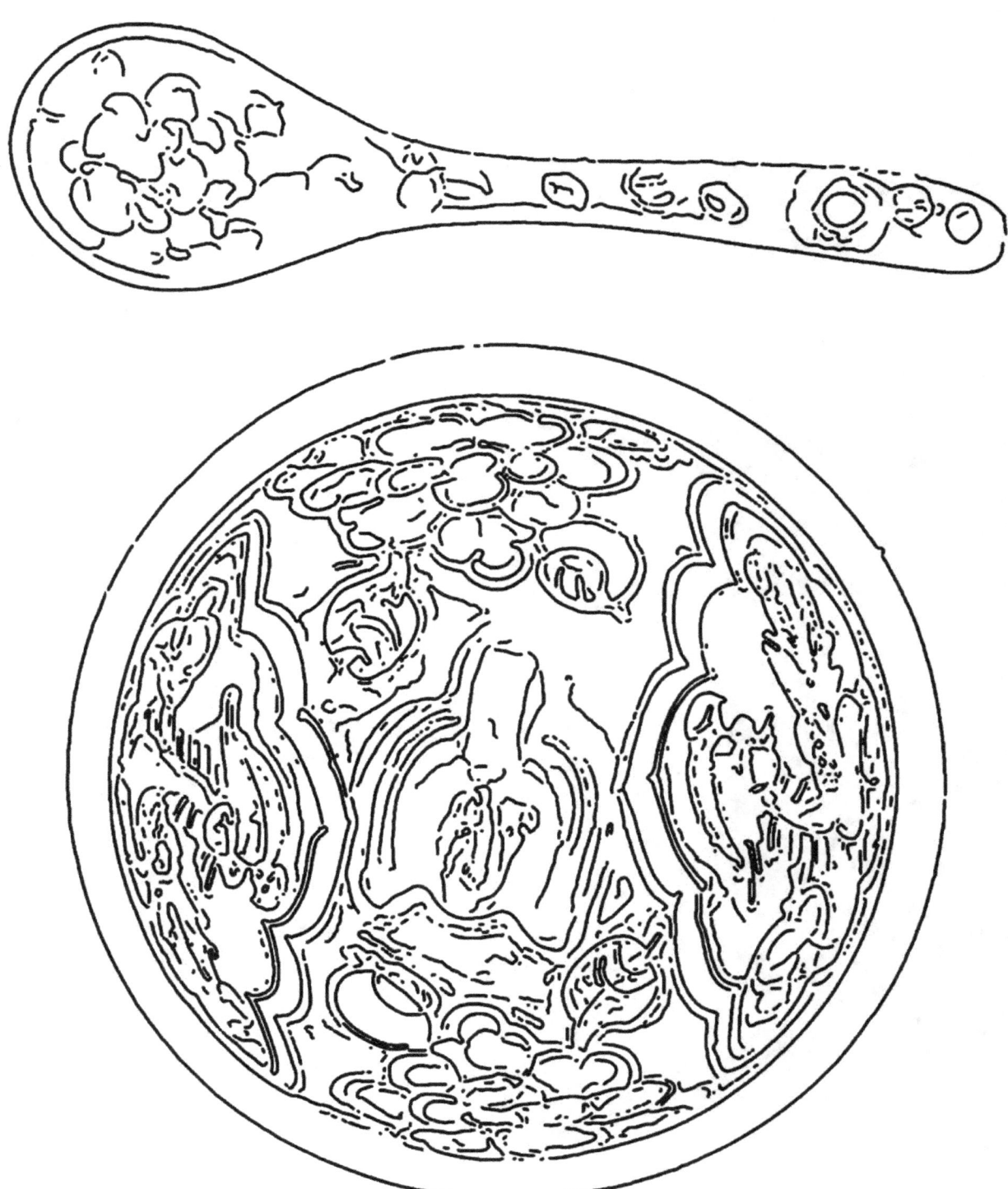

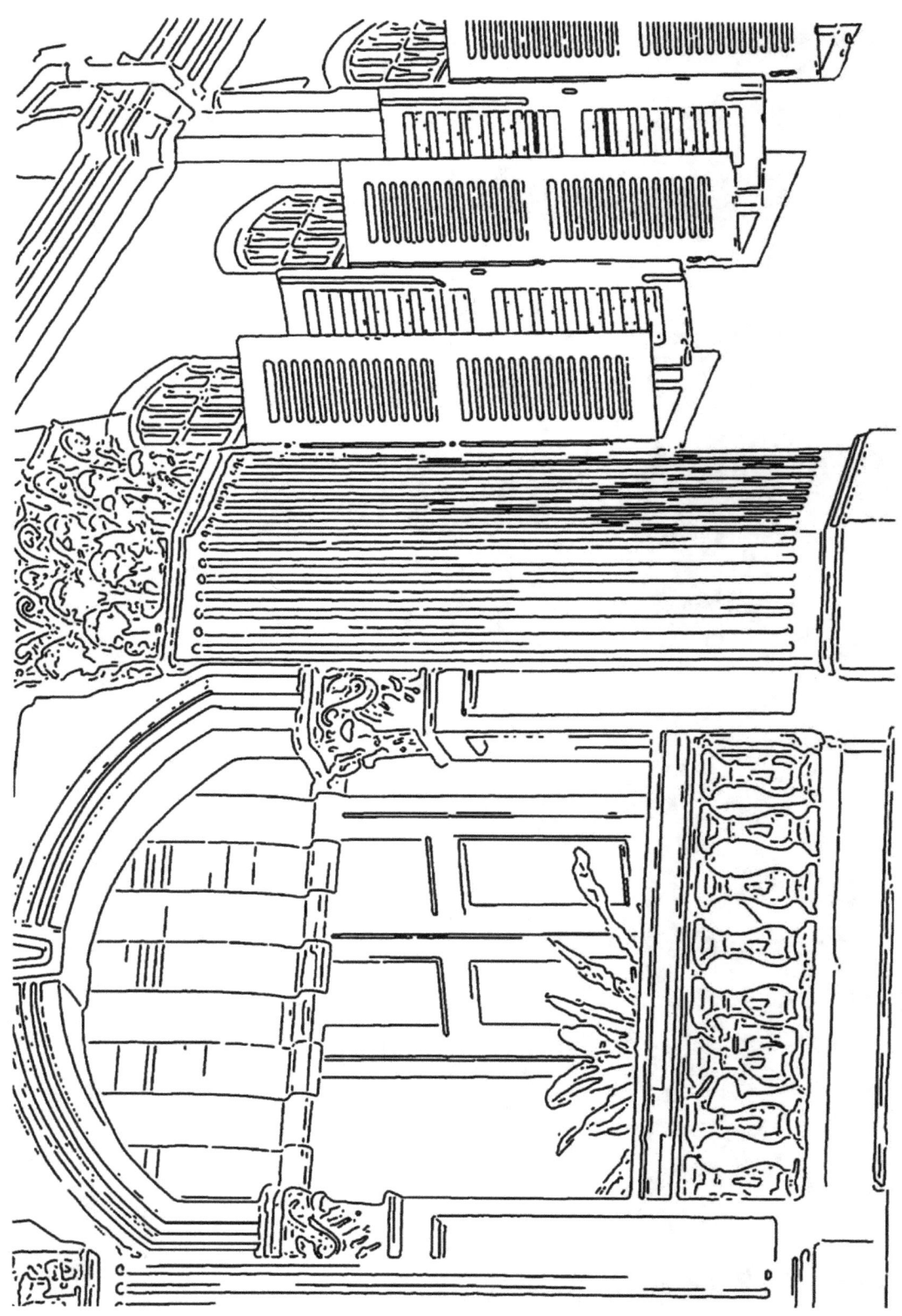

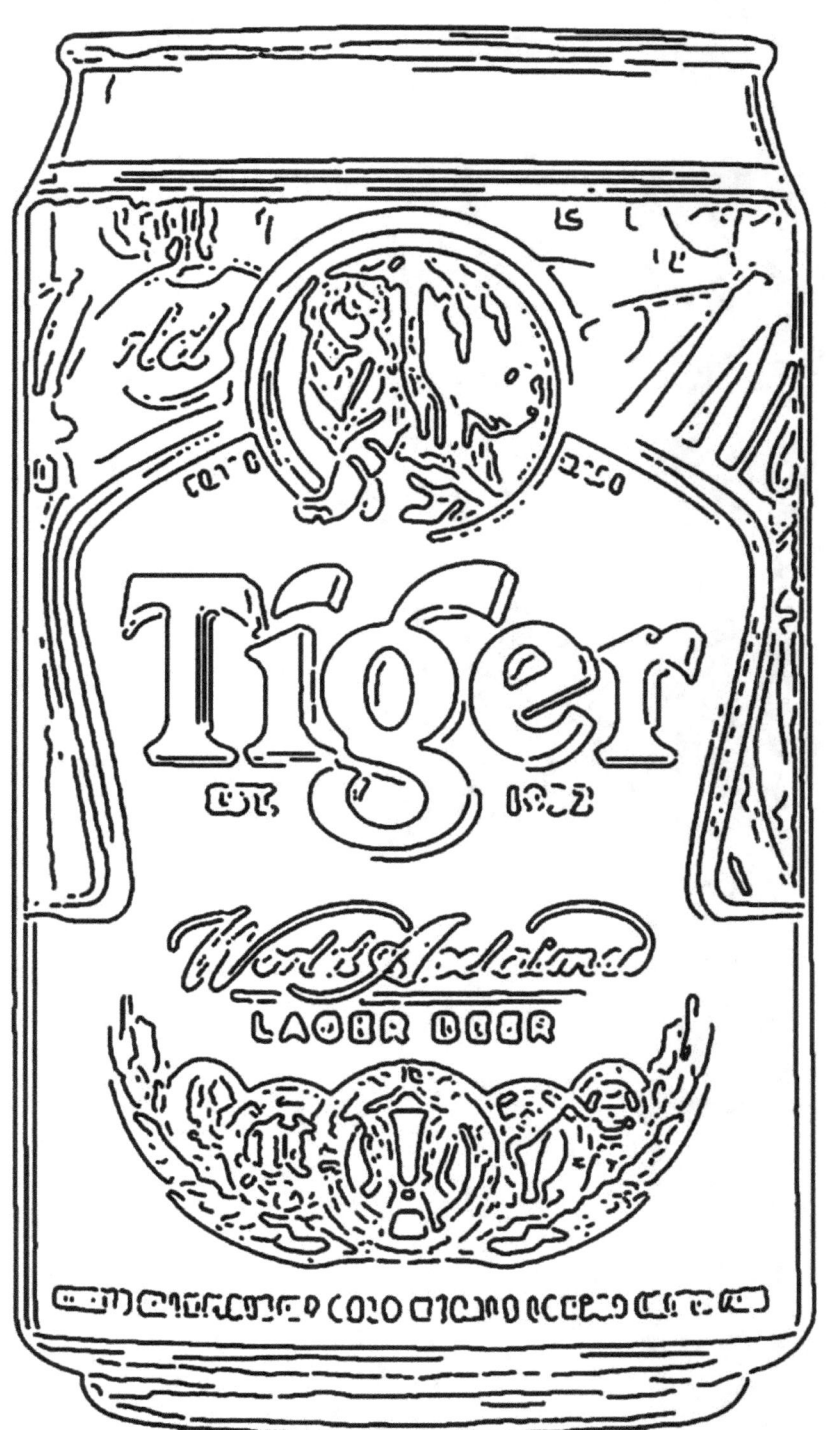

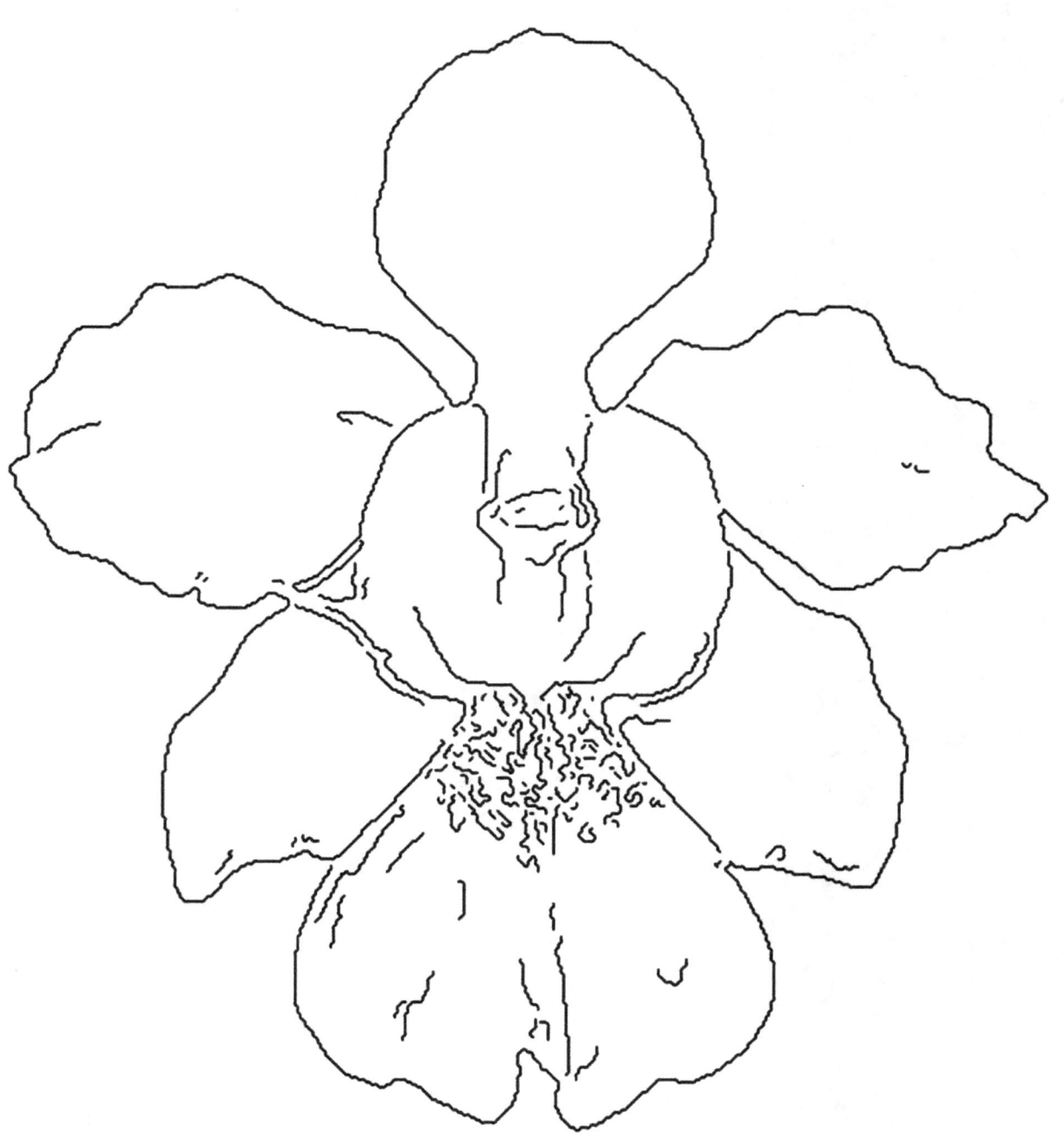

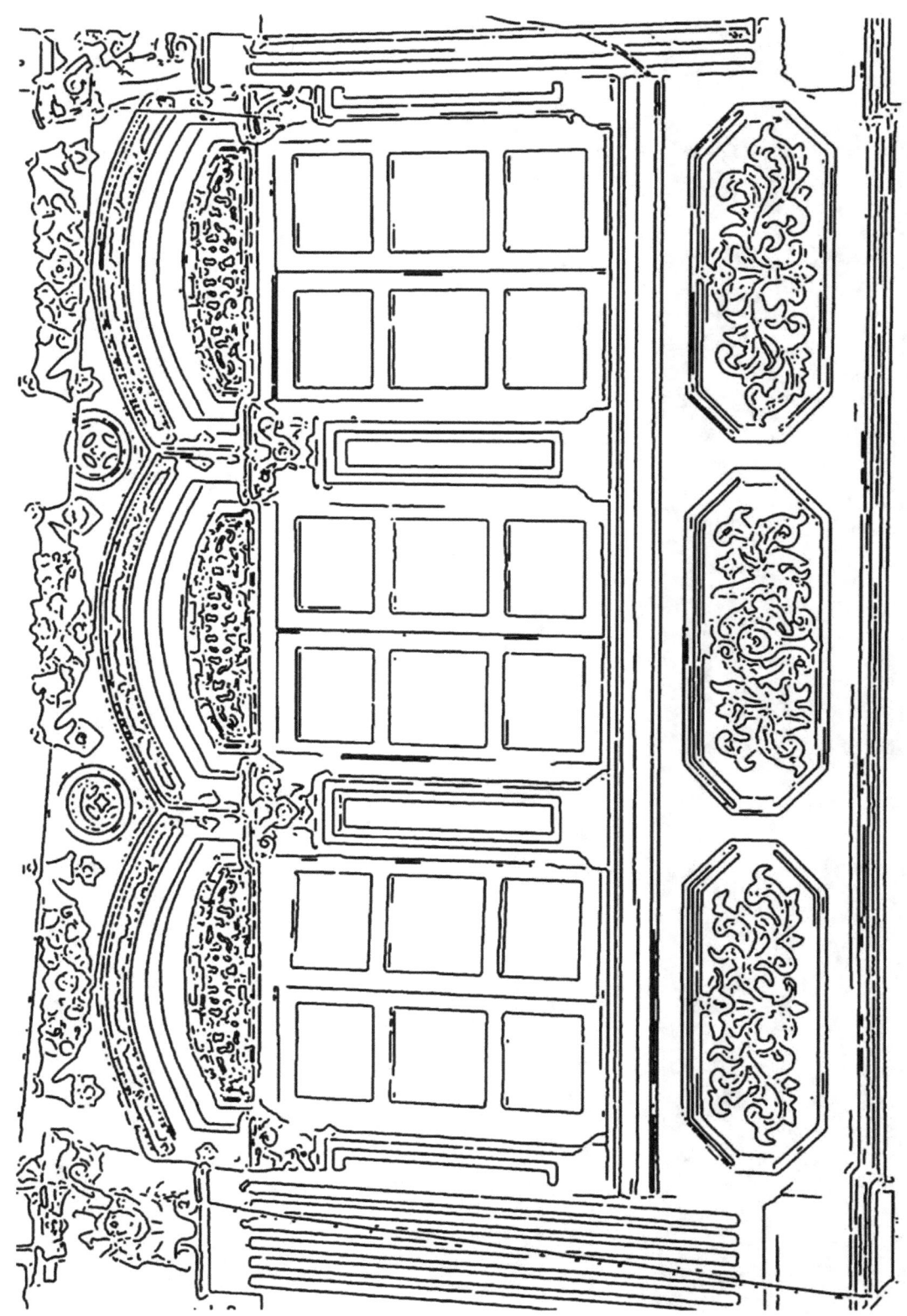

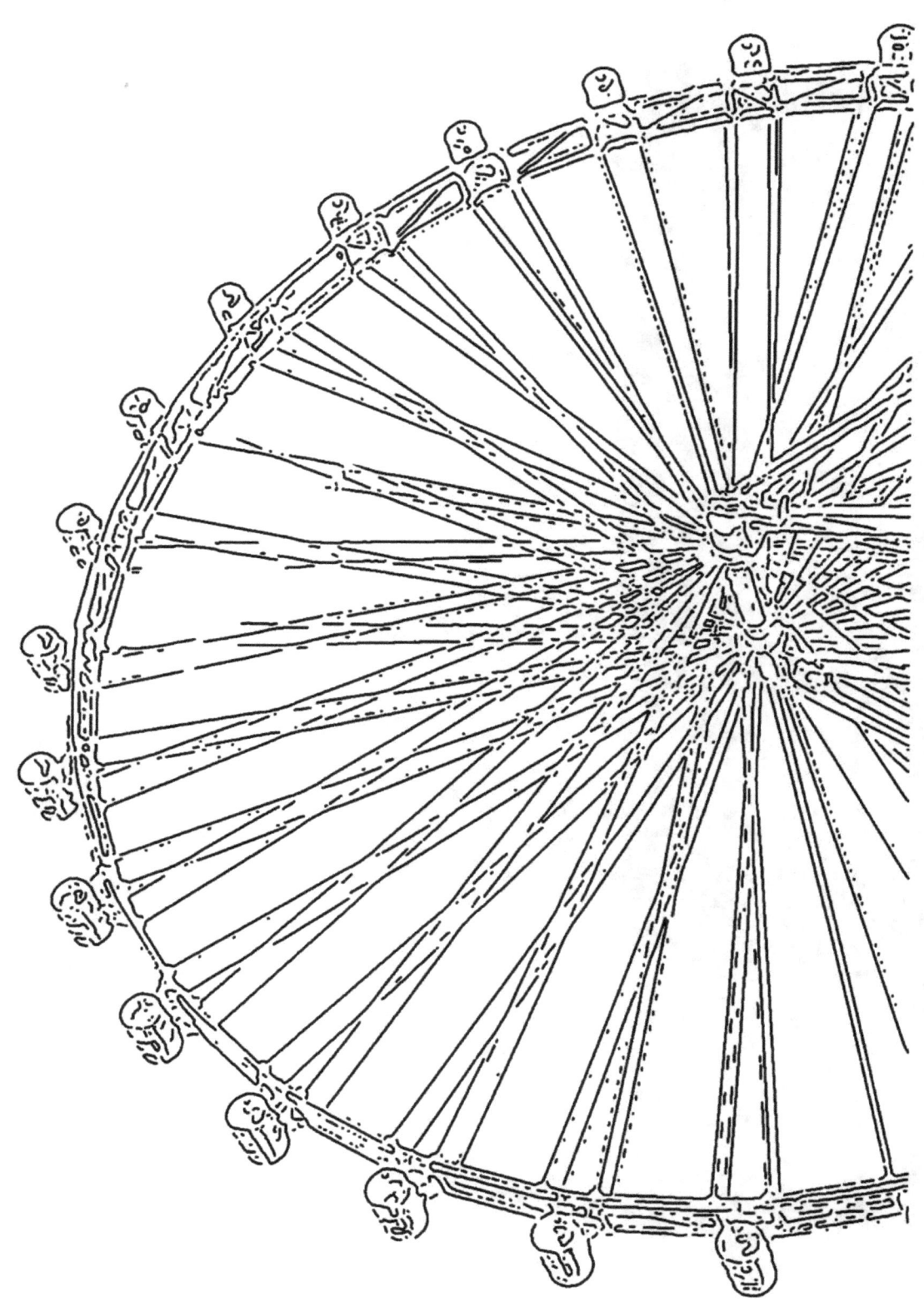

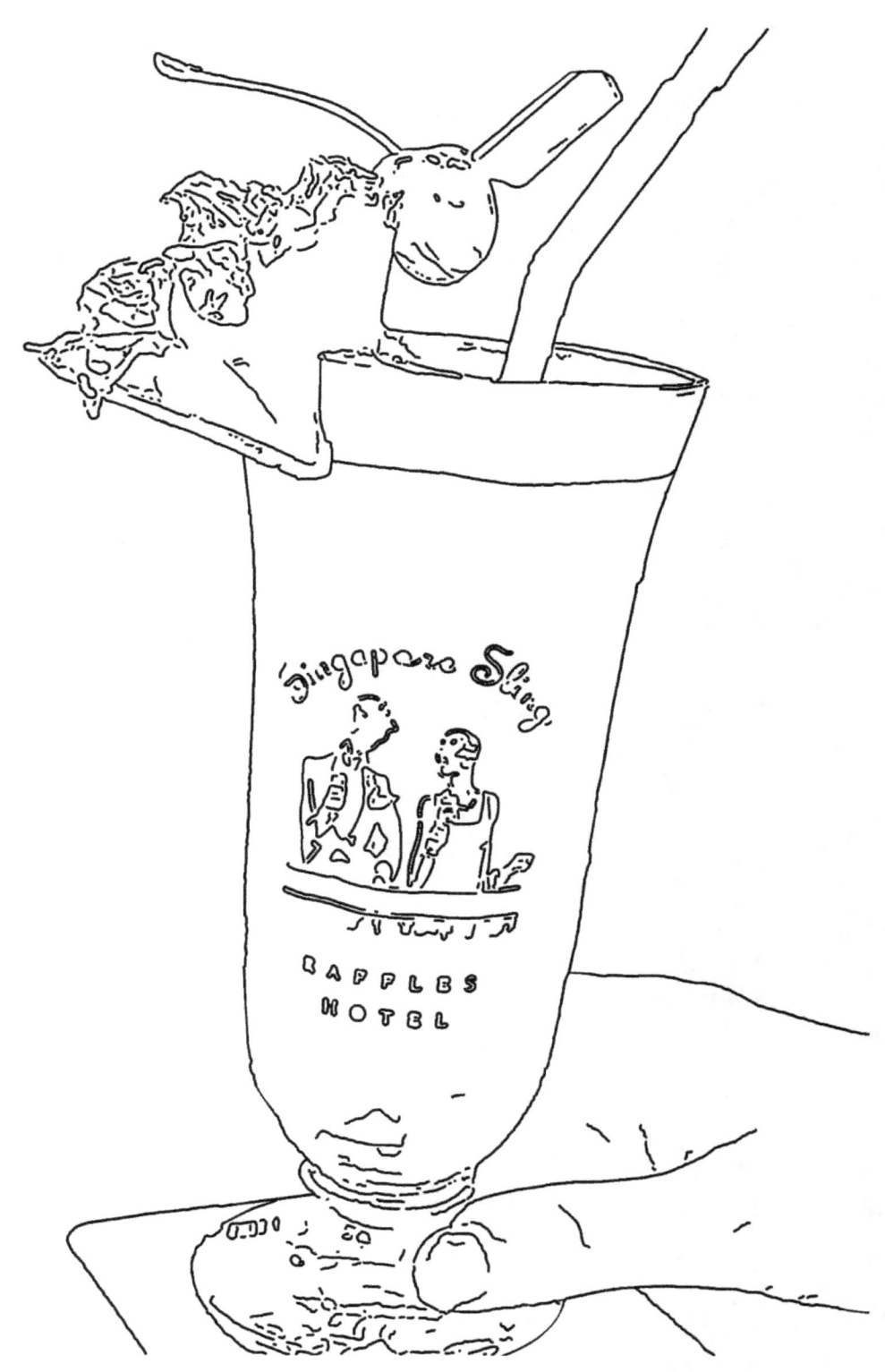

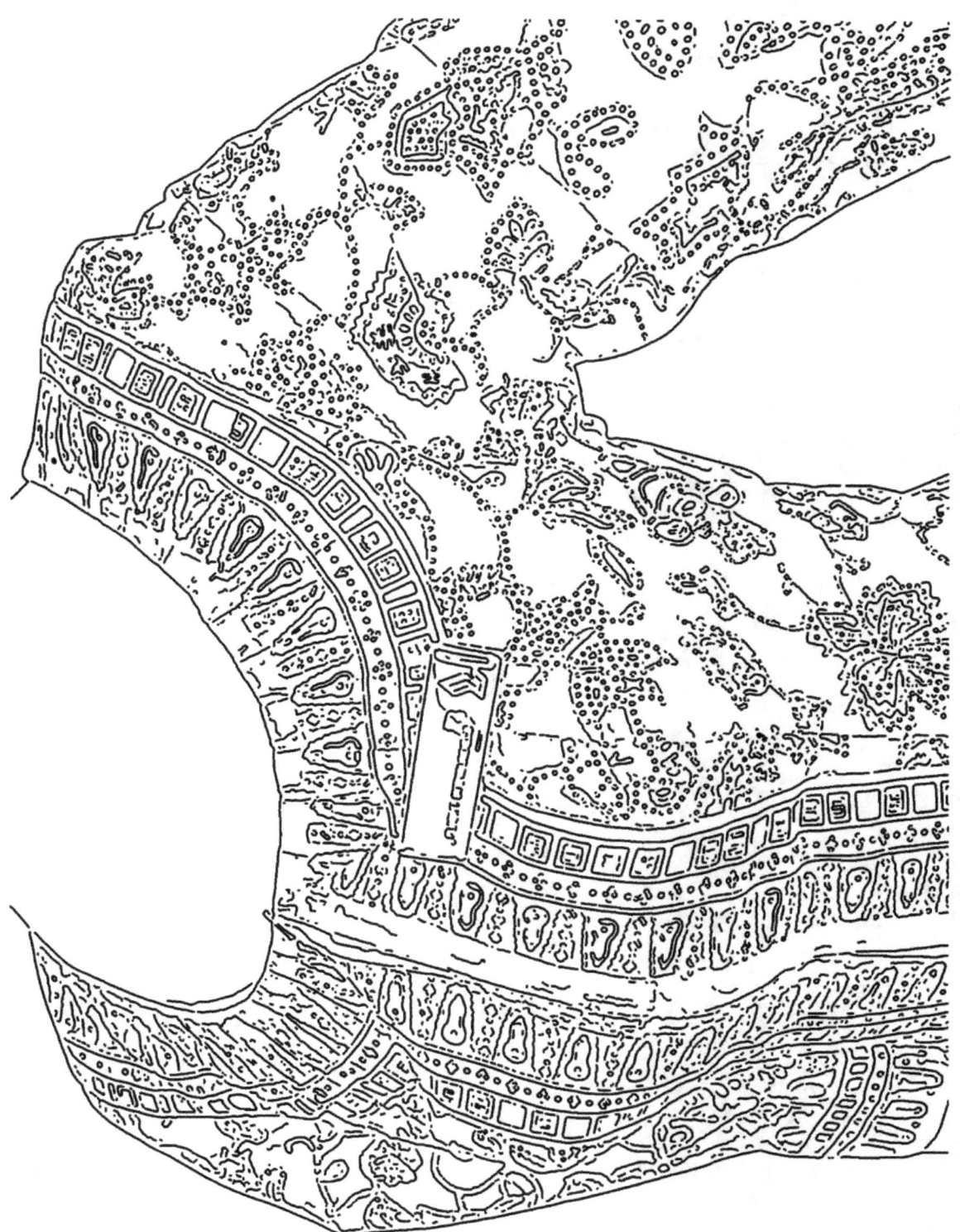

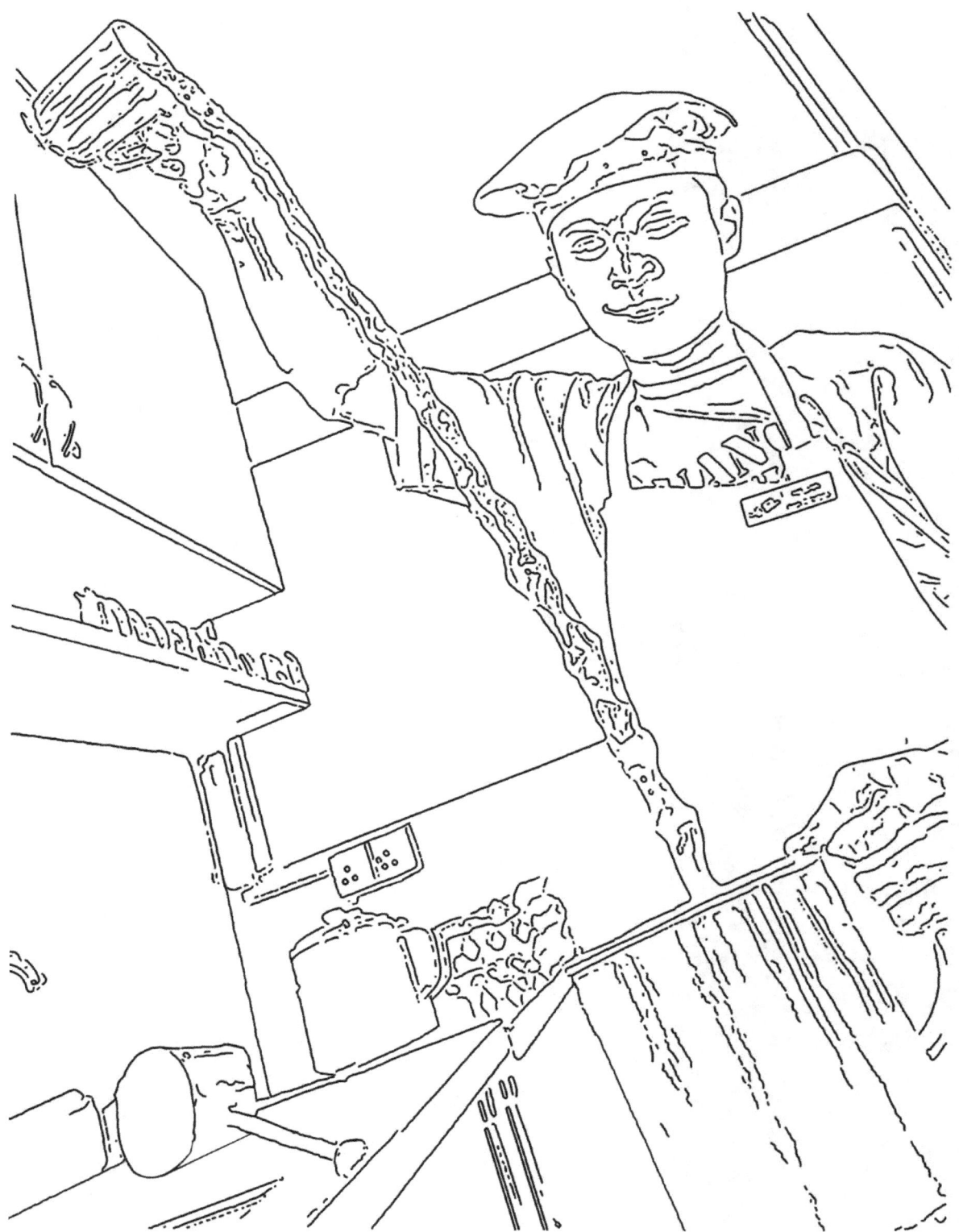

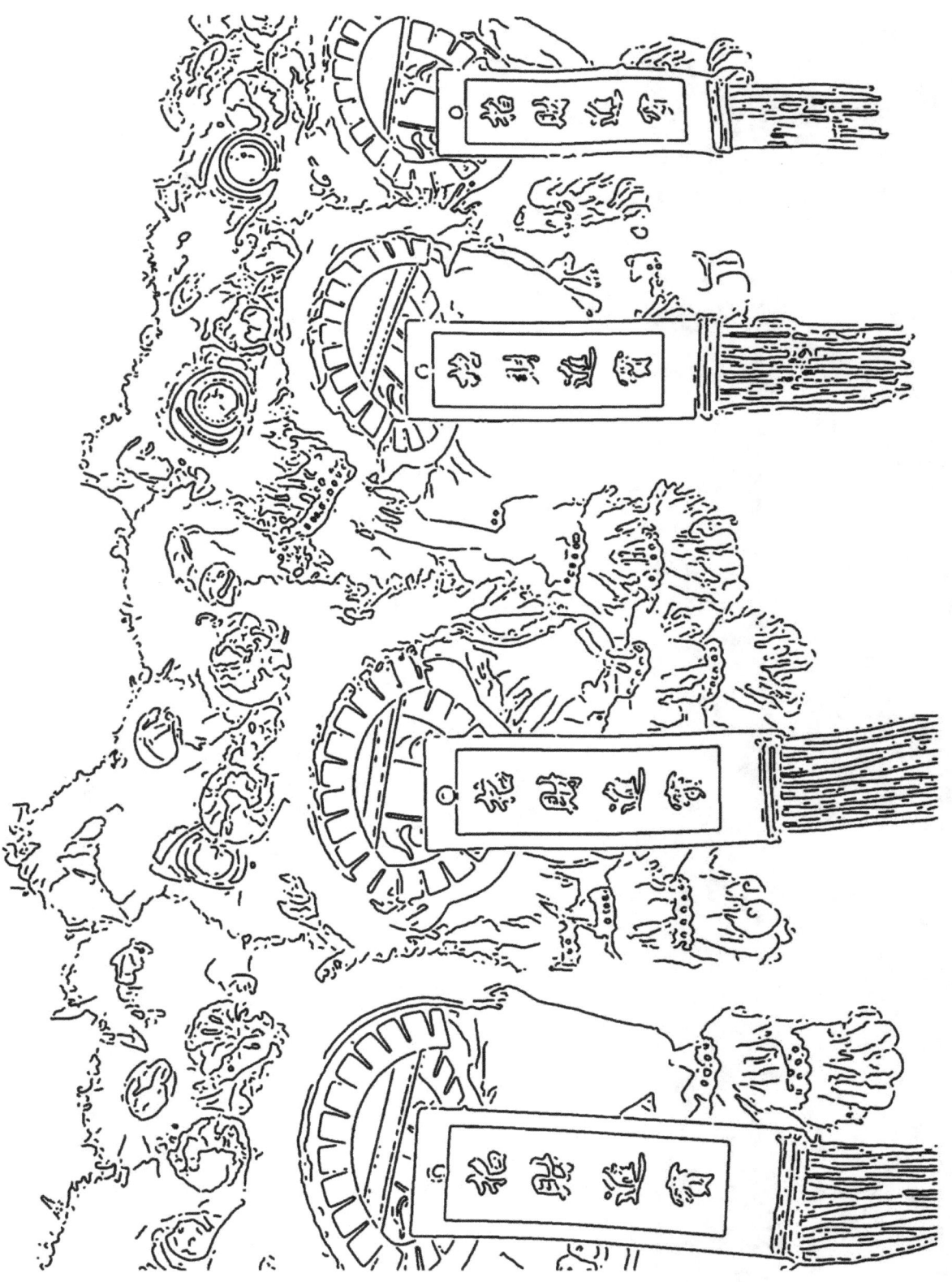

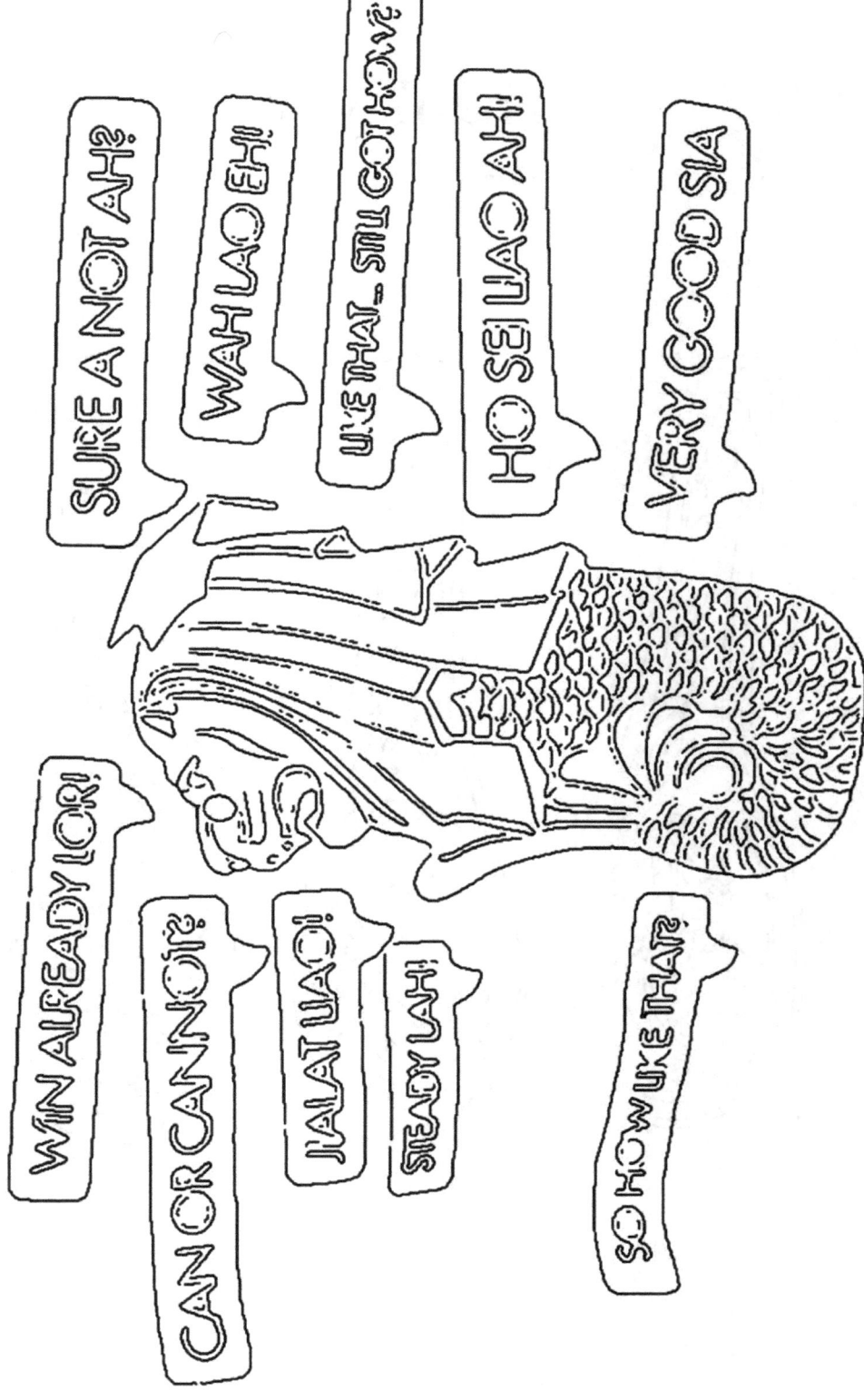

Thank you

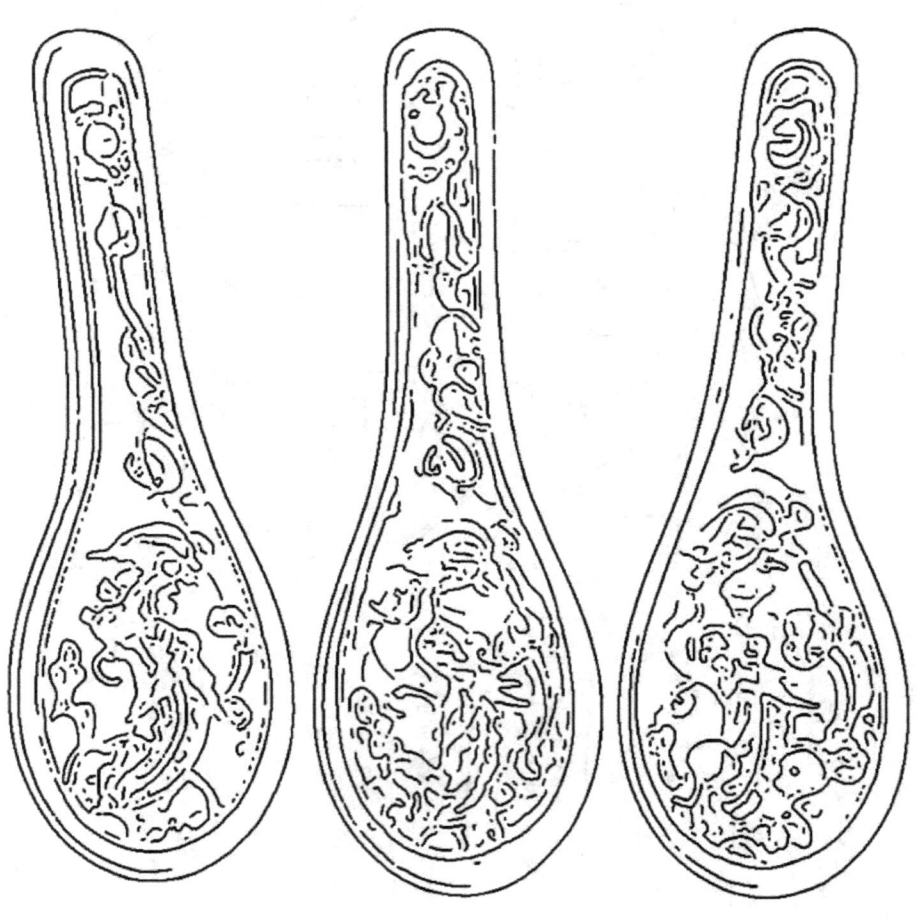